bookmarked.

Cortney VanLiew

BookLeaf Publishing

India | USA | UK

Presentation by *BookLeaf Publishing*

Web: www.bookleafpub.com

E-mail: info@bookleafpub.com

ISBN: 9789358313987

First edition 2023

to my people: be brave.

PREFACE

I have lived many lives in my short time and writing is how I survived. There are many poems I have read that put my thoughts into words. I have always dreamed of being able to do that for other people. As you read, I hope you find the same and that maybe you also find the survival you are looking for.

bookmarked

Hundreds of books. Thousands of pages.
Millions of words. Each one leaving marks on
my soul.

privilege

There is a certain privilege in knowing that when this ends, I will be heartbroken.
There is also a privilege in being enamored with the experience as you're experiencing it.

nature vs. nurture

I have my father's sense of humor, and also his
anger.
I have my mother's cheek bones, and also her
intensity.
I have my brothers' childhood, and also their
work ethic.
I am a collection of the ones who raised me.

mad.

intensely angry or displeased.
insane.
Two definitions for a three letter word. Both I feel when I think of you. Did I imagine our connection? Did I fool myself into believing that you truly meant it when you said you would always be there? Who am I to be so easy to walk away from? Five years of everything turned into nothing in a single moment. Why didn't I get an explanation? Why didn't I deserve the truth?
You make me mad. You made me mad.
I don't hate you, I don't think I am capable. But sometimes, I think it would be easier if I did.

the lake

There is a place hidden up in the trees, a place
where I go to hide.
There is a feeling I get when I am out on the
water, a feeling of unbelievable power.
There is a way that I am at the lake, a way of
existence that I adore.
I am carefree, I am calm, I am complete.

cote de roses

Sometimes I wish I could liquify, and sink into a
pretty little empty bottle of wine. I would just sit
on the shelf. Beautiful. Untouched. Unbothered.
I could catch the light as someone picks me up
to admire me. I could warm in the right pair of
hands. I could cool down in the fridge awaiting a
glass.
Someone could save me for a special day or sip
on me every night. I'd be there in the back of
their mind all day. I'd be needed. I'd be
cherished. I'd be adored.
These are the things I should be now.
These are the things I will be one day.

the loss of a friend

I can forgive you for walking away, but I cannot excuse the lack of an explanation.

intimacy

They asked me about intimacy and my thoughts
strayed to you: the way you grabbed my elbow
as I drove you home, the look you gave me as
you brushed the tears from my eyes, the peace I
felt with my head in your lap and your fingers in
my hair.
It doesn't make sense, to think the name of
someone whose lips have never touched mine.

haiku

with you next to me,
I listen to the rain fall.
pure adoration.

Belief

Everyone needs something to believe in.
God, the Universe, other people.
Whatever it is, everyone needs something to
hold on to, something to devote themselves to.
It's the belief that keeps them moving, that keeps
their world turning.
Belief, such a small word for such a powerful
feeling.

LOVE

Leaving me standing there as you drove away.
Our memories are the only thing left to share.
Violent thoughts run through my head.
Even now, my heart breaks at your name.

Is this how love is supposed to be?

chaos and art

There are words and phrases swirling around my head. Constantly twisting and turning and running into one another. It is no wonder I always have a headache. One with a pain in my temple, one that squeezes my skull, one that muddles all of the pieces of my brain into mush. Some of these phrases I have made up, others are stolen from pages of a book or the conversation of strangers. All of them make up me.

If you were to string them out and weave them together, you would see they are molded into my outline. You would see them create the wrinkles on my forehead, my long, dark eyelashes, the bump of my nose, the scars on my lip and my chin.

Slowly, as you make up sentences, you'll see my body take shape. You'll smile as you see "chaos and art" stretch out over my fingers and sigh as you read "a girl in need of a hug" plastered across my collarbone.

I am just a collection of words, of letters. I am no more than a book about a woman. I am nothing but mixed up phrases and contradictions.

Am I written in the wrong language? Is that why
I am so quickly misunderstood?
Maybe. Or maybe not.
Surely there will come a time when someone
will take the time to read each and every word.
Someone to make sense of the chaos and
appreciate the art. Someone to cherish me like
their favorite book stories, one the read over and
over and over. Never getting tired of it. Always
noticing something new.
I am an open book. If only someone would come
stay awhile and read it entirely.

Sonora Jo

Your name is the music my heart sings to. A platonic soul mate is still a soul mate, tied together with a string of memories, and love, and dreams. I know I will never find another you; I will hold on to you forever.

to be loved

There is power in the knowledge that someone will always be there, whatever you need.

hidden. but blinding.

I see the stains of you scattered throughout my life.
I see it in the clothes I wear, and the music I listen to, and the candy I eat.
I see it in the window of the restaurant we always ate at. I see it on the volume button of my car stereo. I see it on the couch we sat on everyday watching movies.
I hear it in the lyrics of my favorite songs, the laughter of a stranger, and the sound of my voice as I use all of your best phrases.
I smell it in the uncorked bottle of wine, old clothes you game be, and the passerby's cologne in the grocery store.
I feel it in the ghost of your hands wrapping me in a hug, the rain on my skin, the rough sand beneath my toes.
The stains cover my mind, my body, my soul. Because the stains of you, make the best parts of me.
I see the stains and I smile. Because no matter how you left me, you are still with me.
I wonder though, do you have stains too? Do they make you think of me?

God

Without You, I am nothing. With You, I have everything.

Kuusamo

A little town far away, to teach me who I am.
Away from my people, my life, everything I
have ever known.
Time moving too fast, afraid I am missing out on
life.
Always wondering if this is truly worth it.

space

Sometimes you have to step away from
something to realize how much you love it.

There are…

I have a hundred things I'll never get to tell you. There are times in the day when I pick up my phone to tell you a story before I remember I am not allowed to do that anymore. There are moments with a strange sense of deja vu where I know exactly what you would have said, but I will never hear your voice again. There are instances where my heart aches for a moment of how we used to be and I know I need to stop the pain before it breaks me.

A sense of home

They say home is where the heart is, but my
heart is split in different pieces.
A piece lives with you, down in the warmth. A
place of nostalgia and dreams.
A piece lives in a little town in Finland. A place
of destiny and uncertainty.
A piece lives in the house I grew up in. A place
of memory and feeling.
A piece lives with my family. A place of love
and necessity and belonging.
A piece was lost to an old friend. The rest of my
heart will always call out to it.
How can I have so many homes? Will I ever
have an unwavering sense of home?

An ode to my people

The reason I live. The reason I breathe. The reason I love.